WET DREAMS

By
Tiffany "Tip" Taylor

"Spreading my pages for the world to see."

Wet Dreams by Tiffany Taylor

Wet Dreams by Tiffany Taylor

Printed in the United States of America

ISBN: 978-0-9910964-0-4

Edited & Formatted by: Shani Greene- Dowdell

Front and Back cover design: Nayberry Publishing Assistance

Contact Info: Wheatieb@yahoo.com | Facebook

Wet Dreams by Tiffany Taylor

Preface

Wet Dreams is a collection of poems written about stories told by my friends. Whenever I had deep conversations with my close friends, the dialogue would lead to intimacy. We would talk about our fantasies. They would talk about the men that they had encountered and their nights of passion. Even though sometime some of the conversations made my face turn red, I enjoyed them. This book is a candid peek into those conversations.

I hope you have fun reading this book as much as I have writing it.

Best,
Tiffany Taylor

About the Author:
Tiffany "Tip" Taylor is a native of Opelika, AL. She started writing poetry in the 3rd grade. From there, her love of writing began to grow. Tiffany's writing include, Truly into Poetry and Thoughts from My Pen published in 2010 and 2012, respectively. Tiffany also enjoys writing music lyrics, children books, and short stories.

Wet Dreams by Tiffany Taylor

Wet Dreams by Tiffany Taylor

WARNING: I am not responsible for any pregnancies or heart attacks this book might cause!!! ☺☺☺

Wet Dreams by Tiffany Taylor

Eleven Years

Eleven years of wanting and waiting
Going over and over in, my mind contemplating

The feeling built up for so long
It feels so right, it could be wrong

Think about all the time we spent together
Never made love, although we love each other

Emotions overflowing, bodies intertwine
Spirits so close, you can damn near read my mind

Want to plan it out, make sure everything goes right
Want to hear sultry screams in the middle of the night

No phone call. No Interruptions
No time for sleep. Gotta keep it comin'

I want it missionary, so I can feel you inside
Then I want to get on top when it's time to ride

Can't stand the pain of not being able to touch you
Ever since we met, I always knew I loved you

Want it against the wall and in the shower
Want our bodies intertwined hour after hour

I want it on the couch and the balcony
When my lips touch your dick,

Wet Dreams by Tiffany Taylor
I want you to cum for me

I want to sit on your face,
So you can taste my sweet nectar
Making love to you couldn't be better

My body is calling your name, so come and get it
I want you and I'm not ashamed to admit it

Our day to reconnect is coming and coming soon
Together we will be heard like music filling a room

It may only be one time
But the feeling will last forever
I've waited for eleven years
So our time is now or never

Anytime and Anyplace

When I am in the mood
I don't care where
I want to make love
Right then and there

I don't want to look
For a private place
All I need is a
Little bit of space

Desperately needing
You to get me off
Take the time and
Show me whose boss

I can have an audience
I don't care who sees
I can do it in private
Or public with such ease

Ass tooted in the air
Stripped down bare
If someone sees me
Fuck it, I really don't care

As you hit it from the back
I holler, "Oooh shit, right there"
I could care less if people
Give us a blank stare

If you want to see me

Wet Dreams by Tiffany Taylor

Ride his dick like a rodeo
Grab some popcorn
And I'll put on a show

Ladies, you can learn my technique
Even write that shit down
I do things that'll eventually
Have your man coming around

Don't try to stop us
We won't slow down
When my clothes come off
It's going down

Take your phone out
Go ahead take a pic
Watching us fuck is
Like watching a porno flick

For all I care
You can join the fun
If you're not too scared
And want to get up and run

I like it anytime any place
Especially when I'm horny
We can turn this viewing party
Into one big ass orgy

So when you see us
Know your eyes are not being misled
Sit and enjoy for a while
As I give him the best head

As our bodies separate

Wet Dreams by Tiffany Taylor

Vision of pleasure can't be erased
I hope you enjoyed our version
Of anytime anyplace

He Made Me Tap Out

I came across something
That really got a hold of me
Something so strong
It had me on my knees
Bent over with my ass in the air
The way this man was hitting it
I wouldn't even move on a dare
I wanted it again and again
I could feel him so deep
That nigga had me screaming
His name as I gripped the sheets
Hair flinging wild
Face plastered with a smile
I couldn't say a word
The only thing that would leave
My lips were grunts and moans
The way a grown man puts it down
Is what I was shown
Couldn't focus
Mind in a total blur
Any woman in her right mind
Getting this loving would concur
It was good until about 15 minutes in
When to my body's chagrin
He wanted to do it again
This time he wouldn't let up
Laying that love stick on me good
Something tells me I shouldn't
Have brought my ass over here
I've never felt torture like this

Wet Dreams by Tiffany Taylor
Didn't know dick could be so good
To keep his dick as a souvenir,
Man I wish I could
Thirty minutes later
I needed a break
I was about to tap out
Because he was wearing my ass out
Not only was my breathing heavy
My pussy had taken a beating too
He was drilling so good
My ass had a permanent tattoo
When he finished, he asked
"You ready for round two?"
I laughed knowing he had to be joking
I said, "Are you kidding me?
I thought you were through."
He assured me that he had
Plenty more lovemaking to do
Before the night was over
I needed a lifeguard
'Cause this man was ready
Sitting on the edge of the bed
Dick on hard
Before the end of the night
I was tapped out
And pleased in every way
He sexed me up, down, left and right

As Long As it Gets Wet

Most men could give a shit
About what you have on
Or the way you wear your hair to bed
They don't care if your underwear match
They only want pussy they can catch
Cute toes, manicured nails
All that stuff can go to hell
For all a man cares
You could be fresh out of jail
You can do a sexy teddy
But it's coming right off
If you were straight naked
You would be better off
You can have a big belly with no ass
Have a shape of an hourglass
Bald head with a string of hair in the middle
As long as you are giving up a little
He won't care what you look like
You can bet the only thing
He is worrying about is will it get wet?

Between a Dick and a Hard Place

I like the way they fit
In my undercarriage
Even though one takes up
More space than the other
Neither is talking about marriage
The sex is good from both
And they know
I like having choices every night
They both have skills
That I constantly yearn for
They both make my body feel different
Yet, the loving is always consistent
It's my desire to play with fire
I like having my cake
And eating it too
Only one thing that can sweeten
The deal is having my cake eaten by two
It's like having all of your
Favorite foods at the same time
But it's not like I'm doing
Them at the same time
Only the one who can satisfy my appetite
Feed and satisfy this hunger of mine
The longer I do this, the more I enjoy it
So feelings can't be caught up
Because I refuse to give up one or the other
I'm fucking two men, just not at the same time
Some may think I'm out of my mind
To put myself in this situation
But I don't love them, only dick
To whom I am committed

Black Thunder

Damn was the first thing that I said
When I saw the man with the shinny baldhead
He was built like a statue over six feet tall
The last time I saw a man like him I couldn't recall
He had bulging biceps and six-pack abs
His ass looked like something you'd want to grab
He turned around and I damn near wet myself
I had to tell my pussy, "Girl control yourself"
When he walked over to me and said "Hi"
I was in such shock that I couldn't reply
He said, "Nice to meet you
My name is Black Thunder"
My mind immediately began to wonder
Was his dick big and was it sweet?
It took all my might not to touch and see
I finally said "Hi and nice to meet you too"
My eyes were stuck on him like glue
He asked my name and I said "T.I.P."
Then, he kissed my hand ever so gently
He pulled me by the hand and said, "Lets go fuck"
The rest is in limbo
Because that's when I woke the hell up

A Waste of Damn Time

You said you wanted me, so I gave all of me to you.
Why is it you act like you didn't know what the fuck
to do?
Is this your first time? Are you new to this?
There is something in life that you obviously missed.
Do I need to give you a lesson?
Do I need to give you a how to fuck session?
Before we start, you do know that foreplay is involved
Or is that problem that I should solve?
You are acting like this is the first time you have seen
a pussy.
You know that thing between my legs that's kind of
cushy.
You can touch it. It doesn't bite.
If you treat her good, she'll do you right.
Piss her off and that bitch will close.
Then, you'll have to find another place to stick your
hose.
Do you even know what hole your dick goes in?
Or do I need a checkered flag to guide you in?
Are you there yet 'cause I don't feel a thing?
I think there is something wrong with your dingaling
Why are you huffing and puffing? It's only been one
minute.
It is not like it's the first time you've been in it.
Three minutes pass and you're already done.
This is not what I call fun.
A waste of my damn time, you coming over here.
I have had more fun-watching cartoon and drinking a
beer.

I roll over and fall fast asleep like you knocked it out
the park.
Even though you didn't even ignite the slightest
spark.

Bondage

I got whips and sex swings, ropes and cuffs
I like to whip until I had enough
I've got hoods, leashes, and bondage sheets
I like to tie you up and bring out my inner freak
If you think you can handle it, come and get it
Trust and believe you won't regret it
I like being in control, total dominatrix
I'll see you in my room, if you think you can take it
I don't need you squirming. You need to stay still
And let me how you like my bondage skills
I like to blind my victims and make them feel invalid
Give yourself to me completely committed
In my secret room in the secret chamber
I become the ultimate entertainer
Remain quiet and only speak when I say so
I'm in command. It's time for you to let go
You will be spanked if you have been bad
I'll put you over my knee and you will be glad
When I give you something that you've never had
Make you beg for more and crawl on your knees
I'm the one that holds the keys
To your sexual pleasures of dripping hot cum
Whippings of pleasure until you are numb
You get almost to the point of ecstasy and
Then I pull it all away
And when I do there is nothing you can say
Give you a little bit of pain but make it feel real good
Keep you always, oh I
wish I could
But as always our little game must come to an end
Until next time, stay sexually free. We will play again.

Can You Make It Wet

Let me ask you something
Can you turn me on
Make my pussy wet
Make it jump on its own
Make me lick my lips
When you arrive
Make me want you
In between my thighs
Can you make me stress
Because I want you all the time
Make me go crazy
And find the nearest wall to climb
Can you make it wet without licking it
Can you make me cum
Without even sticking it
If you can do that
Then you've got skills
I'll bet money on
How good you can make me feel
Can I think about you and feel
The wetness cum down
I might just have to put
Your ass on lockdown
Can you make it squirt
Can you make it gushy
Can you turn the water
Faucet on in this pussy?

Can You Make Me Cum?

A few have tried
All have failed
They just could not prevail
In making me cum
No matter what position
They couldn't make it happen
No matter how long
They attempted to please me
Still nothing...
Not even a toy could do the job
And when we were done
I felt like I'd been robbed
Making me cum
Is like being in the Olympics
You may win in all other sports
But when you get to the main event
You end up last
I've had small dick
Big dick and all in between
Bad lovers, good, and great
It's not as easy as it may seem
It's a challenge to make me cum
Are you up for it?

Pussy Sampler

Pussies are like a buffet
I have to taste different ones
To see what I like best
I like all types
Shaved or not
It doesn't matter what color
If I could, I would line them up and
Go down the line tasting
Them one by one

I wish I could go to
A restaurant serving pussy
As an appetizer
I would taste a little of each
Enjoying each appetizer
I'd eat all day
I'm not picky
As long as it's clean and right
I could have pussy
Morning, noon, and night

Pussy for breakfast, lunch and dinner
If I could, I would have pussy lollipops
In all different flavors
I would lick them nonstop
Being this satisfied is not cheating
It's just a sensual taste test
Some women pass the test
While others don't

I keep a little black book
The phone numbers and names

All have a rating for the pussies
Not all men can do this
The way that I do
It takes a man with a
Special type of tongue
And thank goodness for me
A sample that this man
Just will not do

Damn, "Do You Ever Cum?"

We've been going at it for an hour
And I just want to know one thing:
"Damn, did this dude drink an energy drink?"
We've been fucking for so long
That I can't even think
When I asked him, "Have you cum yet?"
He said no and I started to regret
That I asked him over in the first place
If He would know that I was tired
If he could see the expression on my face
My pussy was taking a beating
Poor thing crying out for help
A dick like this she ain't ever felt
I came so many times that I lost count
With anticipation building, I know when he comes
It's going to be a huge amount
Forget my eyes rolling back
They've rolled all the way around
He gives a new meaning to putting it down
Got me grabbing sheets and grabbing pillows
When will he cum?
I guess only he knows
He wants me to call his name and talk dirty
The only thing I can say is "Lawd have mercy!"
Twenty different positions
In every which a way, I've been had
Loving this long, a girl should be glad
Well, I'll be glad when he is done
I'm not in shape to be in some of these positions
So I advised him, "Hurry up, catch a feeling and cum."

Deep Throat

Getting you hard from soft
Getting you excited as I blow you off
Take you in and get you nice and wet
Give you something you won't forget

Make your toes curl and your eyes roll back
You're acting like a maniac
You can't believe this, not at all
As I suck you good and play with your balls

Look you in the eyes while I take you all in
You feel a subtle tingling on your skin
Your big dick may hit the back of my throat
But a great gag reflex I have, so I don't choke

You grab the sheets and tighten your grasps
I can tell you are ready to blast
You say, "Baby I hope you're ready for some
Open wide 'cause I'm about to cum"

Even If My Husband Knows

I have a secret that's not really a secret
Because my husband knows I like to swing
I like fucking men and women
It doesn't make a difference
As long as pussy and dick is involved
I fuck whom I want and he does too
As long as he comes back home to me
Sometimes, I might be in the same room
While he is ravaging another woman
We might even be doing the same person
My husband doesn't fuck men
He says that's going to far
But I'm always down for a little ménage trios
It puts a little spice in our marriage
Keeps it nice and fresh
We're well protected
Yeah, we are freaky, not crazy
But we take pleasure in knowing
A new body every weekend
And never knowing what we are going to get
We have our favorites who we like to call
But when it comes to fucking someone new
I'm like a kid in a candy store
I like exploring new bodies
And how they respond to my touches
I like making them feel like
I'm the best they ever had
All my husband wants is a one-night stand
We form no relationships
Just a freak feast to satisfy
Our appetite for sex

Fuck All The Foreplay

Fuck all that foreplay
I want the dick now
You said you'd make me cum
You gave a vow
I like it missionary
When I want you close
With every stroke
I want an overdose
I want it slow first
Grind on me
Until you are about to burst
Make me scream your name
Put your face in my neck
Breath within the creases
Deep within

After the slowness of your rhythm
I want you to speed it up
Oh, yeah...
You know the way I like to fuck
Make my head hit the headboard
Make me beg for those
Blow my back out moves
Flip me over and hit it from the back
Give my hair a pull
And my ass a smack
As I feel each strike
Against me leading to the ultimate "O"
Yes, baby!
Make my cum

Cum down like rain
After this, I'll want another round

When we are done
Don't tell me you are tired or worn out
Because it's my turn to ride you out
Hold on for one hell of a ride
I'm going to ride that dick
With a whole lot of pride
We'll make the bed move
We'll make the bed squeak
Fucking until fucking is tired of fucking
Removing all of the sheets
I love the way you feel deep inside
As I ride you so hard
It bring tears to my eyes
So like I said, Fuck all that foreplay
I want the dick now
You said you'd make me cum
You gave a vow
When my eyes roll back into my head
I understand how
You are a man of your word
I'm about to cum now

One Night Stand

I met you at the club, while I was out with my girls
The night I decided to wear my necklace with the
matching pearls

I was sitting at the bar when you arrived
Wearing the short skirt that came up to my thighs

You didn't see at first, but I was checking you out
I knew immediately I wanted to try you out

After an hour of partying, you saw me eyeing you
From the expression on your face, I knew you
understood what I wanted to do

So you came over to the bar and asked my name
You asked if I was interested in playing a little game

I said, "Of course I like to have a little fun."
You said, "Okay let's make a little run."

My girls said, "Girl you're crazy for going with him."
I left the party behind, even a wine glass filled to the
rim

I followed you in my ride back to your place
On the way, I was imagining your cum on my face

When we got to the house, you pulled me in
You had a nice living room and that is where we
began

Wet Dreams by Tiffany Taylor

You pulled off my skirt and then my blouse
I could tell that you were instantly aroused

You started with a simple kiss on the neck
It wasn't long before you worked your way to my chest
Planting your lips for a suck tease on my breasts

Your tongue licked gently around my nipple
As you touched my areola, it started to tickle

You took my hand and led me to the bedroom
You said you wanted to make me see the stars and
the moon

I sat on the bed and removed your pants
And your dick began to do the rising dance

I put you in my mouth, just a little at first
The way I sucked you, I knew you were going to burst

I relaxed my throat while I took you all in
I almost gagged as spit ran down my chin

You stopped me and laid me back on the bed
You placed my legs apart, as far as they would spread

While running your fingers across my lips
I began to suck gently on your fingertips

Moving downtown, you opened me and licked inside
The satisfied expression on my face I could not hide

When your fingers stroked and played with my clit
I knew then at that moment I would totally submit

Climbing on top of me, you placed a kiss on my neck
You entered me so quickly I didn't expect

One thrust, two thrust – I wanted more
I knew a good fucking was in store

I moaned in your ear to get your full attention
"Baby," I said, "Let's change positions."

I wanted to feel you deep. I wanted it from the back.
As you pulled my hair and gave my ass a smack

When I had my fill, I got on top and went for a ride
Watching your eyes rolled back in your eyelids and hide

You flipped me back over landing on top
And quickly began to thrust nonstop

You thrust and I grinded until we both came
You let out a moan as you screamed my name

After we were done, it was time turn in
And When we woke up the next morning, we did it again

Itty Bitty

If you got a lil' dick
You better learn to eat pussy quick
Ain't nobody got time to
Be foolin' with that lil shit

Hiding behind your balls
Scared to come out
Looking like your balls
Got lips trying to pout

What happen to it
Why is it so small
When you were born
Did something fall off

What's a damn shame
Is that you got robbed
I can't even give your
Ass a nice blow job

How you jack off
You can't use your hand
Your index finger and thumb
Is what's in the plan

Dick so small
Need an implant
The only thing you
Can fuck is an ant

Wet Dreams by Tiffany Taylor

Forget fucking a woman
We won't feel a thing
We'll take a vibrator
Over your tiny dingaling

And when you cum
There's only a drip
You can wipe that shit
Away with a Q-tip

You try to make it look big
By wearing tight jeans
The only thing you doing is
Making your nuts scream

If you got a lil' dick
Go ahead and admit it
Don't be coming to a woman
Like you're going to hit it

Make Up Sex

I've been pissed off
At you for a couple of days
This is the second time
I've asked you to do the dishes
And help out around the house
When I work late
All you say is baby...
The game was on or I feel sleep
Okay I'll put your ass to sleep all right

You know that I'm pissed so you've
Been tiptoeing around the house
Trying not to disturb me
You have some making up to do
It's going to be a long ass time
Before I wash dishes
Or clean the house again

A couple of days go by
And the house starts smelling
You say, *"Baby, the house smells kind of bad."*
I say, *"Yep, I know."*
Not only am I'm not cleaning
You ain't getting none either
Oh, I know you are fiending for it
Because you are always trying to grab me

Wet Dreams by Tiffany Taylor

Knowing that I'm not going to do it
You start cleaning until
Everything is put back into its right place
In two hours, the house is spotless
Not one time do I look at your face
I don't even look up from my book
Eventually, I hear the shower running
Minutes later, you are standing in front of me
With nothing but a towel on

You take the book from my hand
Lead me to the bedroom
And make love to me until
I beg you to stop…but you don't
You say, *"This is make up sex
For all the time you held out."*

Oh, my God
I will never hold out again
He takes my hand and leads me
From the bed and pushed me against the wall
I feel nothing but the pressure of you
As you thrust over and over again
Back to the bed
You take me from the back
Where you finally release
All over my ass
Maybe next time
I'll just do the damn dishes

Midnight Snack

Ummm...
He told me that
I look like a buffet
He wanted to eat me
Like I was a gourmet

He wanted to taste me
'Cause I tasted sweet
He wanted to lick me
Until I grabbed the sheets

But I was tired
Been at work all day
I really, really
Didn't want to play

He said baby relax
And just lay back
All I want is
A midnight snack

I want to see you
Twitch and make you cum
I want to lick you
Until your pussy goes numb

Using both hands
He spread my legs apart
He said my pussy looked
Like a work of art

Wet Dreams by Tiffany Taylor

He wanted to paint my canvas
Using his tongue as the brush
He was going to take
His time, no need to rush

He started with one stroke
Then two and three
It felt so good
He had me moaning off key

OOhhh...
I told him he was the shit
The moment he started
Licking my clit

He said he was hungry
And wanted more
My pussy was what
He wanted to explore

I came in his mouth
Until he was full
With a smile on his face
He had a mouthful

I asked did my pussy
Satisfy his appetite
Like milk did my cum
Do his body right

He said he enjoyed my pussy
And his tongue's embrace
He then went to sleep
With a grin on his face

Morning Love

Love in the morning time
To get your day started right
Even though you made
Love the previous night
Sex in the morning puts
Pep in your step
It doesn't matter how
Well you slept
He whispers in your ear
I want some
Pussy for breakfast
Forget captain crunch
He comes back at twelve
And eats more for lunch
Pussy extra wet
Dick extra hard
Morning breath is
Completely discarded
The warm feeling
That melts like butter
So good in the morning
It makes you stutter
Sex in the morning
Is not unheard of
There is nothing like
That sweet morning love

No Dick Needed

Who said you need
To have a dick to be satisfied
All of my girlfriends can testify
I know how to put it down
Just with my tongue
Have them bitches
Singing a song
Have their lips quivering and
Their legs shaking
They never have to worry
About any baby making
Once I do you
You won't need a man
My tongue will be in demand
No more worrying
About balls on your face
The love that I give
You will embrace

No more worrying about
Will he get a hard on
I can keep you satisfied
All nightlong
In the middle of the night
I will have you talking
Just let my fingers
Do the walking
To find your sweet spot
To make you cum
Lick you so much that
My tongue will be numb

Wet Dreams by Tiffany Taylor
I will make you forget about
Any man that you ever had
Memories of my technique
Will forever be
sketched in your head

Nympho

The purpose of this
Poem is to talk about
Why I'm a nympho
And how it came to be
I was a quiet girl
Always been shy
Never had the nerves
To talk to a guy
Kept to myself
Kept my head in the books
Never really worried about
Any of my looks
Didn't go out much
Didn't have too much fun
I was getting older
My life hadn't begun
Until I met one man
That turned my life around
He waited a while
Before he put it down
And when he did
I was in another world
I felt like a completely
Different girl
He brought a side out
That I didn't know I had
This life lesson isn't taught
By your mom and your dad
He did things to me
That you can't even name

Wet Dreams by Tiffany Taylor

I didn't just call out his first
But his middle and last name
I not only saw the moon and the stars
I saw lil' Martians walking on Mars
He'd smack my ass
And pull my hair
How loud we were
I didn't even care
He had my body shaking
My eyes rolling back
I felt like I was addicted to crack
And I was addicted
But the crack was sex
The only thing I wondered was
Whose dick was next
With just one man
I couldn't get enough
And I realized that
I liked it kind of rough
When I was done with him
I went on to find more
One man...two men
Three and four
I didn't want a relationship
I just wanted to fuck
I could have three at a time
With any luck
No matter where I was
If I wanted a man
I would do him right then and there
That was the plan
Married or single
Black or white
Short or tall
Doesn't matter the height

Wet Dreams by Tiffany Taylor

As long as he is
Able and willing
To give that satisfying feeling
Of a man between my legs
Give me more
Is what I beg
I need much sex
Trying to be nobody wife
A nympho is the way
I live my life

Pussy Monster

I am the pussy monster
My face is always glazed
Ready for the next
Woman to call out my name
My tongue is my weapon
I aim to please
I will make you
Buckle at your knees
Make you grab the sheets
Make your eyes roll back
Make you say ahhh shit
I like it like that
Grab the back of my head
Hold it in place
I love to see the expression
On your face
You tell me that you like it
That you want more
Lick your pussy until
My tongue is sore
I know how you like it
My tongue in deep
And I like to lick it
Because it tastes so sweet
Now turn over and
Let me lick it from the back
In and out your pussy
As you arch your back
Your breathing is getting heavy
You're about to loose it

Wet Dreams by Tiffany Taylor
I put my fingers deep within it
As I continue to lick your clit
And you like the way it hit
Against your pussy
With the long stroke
With my tongue I poke
I like to tickle it
Make it feel good
You know I'm the best
Glad we got that understood

Riding on Top

I feel you sliding in underneath me
My mind and pussy is in disbelief
As you slow grind against my walls
And I hope I don't fall
While riding this mountain of a man
You make me feel like I've gone
To the mountaintop to shout
'Cause I'm about to lose my mind
As you grind
This feeling I've never felt before
I want it more and more
How does it feel, you ask
Hell I can't do nothing but stutter
As your dick slides in and out
Like it been covered in butter
You're hitting every inch of me
Making my eyes roll back
Oh! My! I think I'm turning
Into a nymphomaniac
It has to be a law against
What he's doing to me
They need to lock his ass up
And throw away the key
I've been tipsy before
But not from a dick
He must have had
Liquor in his shit
I woke up the next morning
With a hangover and a headache
The ride I took last night
Was a trip I'd again take

Size Does Matter

I don't care what anyone says
Size does matter
So you can stop
With the chit and the chatter
Saying it's not the size
But the motion of the ocean
I don't know about you
I like a big dick in my potion
Itty Bitty don't do shit for me
It's just too small
I don't want anyone with a dick
Smaller than their balls
All the foreplay in the world
Won't make up for the size
Don't care how much
You lick between my thighs
If I need a magnifying glass
Just to see your shit
I'm going to need for
You to call it quits
Because fucking is
Not your thing
Think of the misery
That lil' thing would bring
No matter how you move
Or how hard you pump
It will feel like you
Getting fuck by a stump
Your poor little dick has
The Napoleon complex

Better entertain a woman with
Something more than sex

Super Dick

I thought I was dreaming
So I rubbed my right eye
That damn thing
Was longer than my thigh
And it was thick too
Just the right size
My eyes were locked in
It had me hypnotized
No wonder he leaned
Over when he walked
And when he spoke
His dick seemed to talk
He started with a tease
As he began to stoke
With that big dick
He was no joke
I squeezed it tight
Wanted to make it mine
I knew that dick had
To be one of a kind
It spoke to me
It was calling my name
What I want to do with it
I wasn't ashamed
I wanted to grab it
Wrap my lips around
And then ride that
Bitch like the Grey Hound
Dick like that I feel it in my gut
Wanted to fuck it
Until it begin to nut

Wet Dreams by Tiffany Taylor

Super dick couldn't do
Anything but satisfy
Made my entire
Body feel electrified

Sweet and Low

If you don't licky, licky
Then you don't sticky, sticky
I want my pussy wet
None of that quicky, quicky

If you cant go sweet and low
Then you're no good for me
Having my pussy licked is
Not just a fantasy

Your tongue has to be thick
And not to rough
And you don't stop until
I get enough

I want it done right
No playing around
It will be your lucky day
If I cum around

You need to start slow
Using nice long strokes
If you do it right
The bed I will soak

Move your tongue in
And out my pussy
Oh that feeling
Does something to me

Wet Dreams by Tiffany Taylor
I'm going to need you
To suck on my clit
Until I start to shiver
And say that's the shit

Lick me so good
Until I push back on the bed
You should get an Oscar
For giving good head

When you look up at me
I want your face to glisten
Your tongue in my life
Is what I've been missing

Put your finger inside
Two at a time
With moves like that
You will blow my mind

Let me sit on your face
While your tongue tickles me
You'll find that is the best
Position to release me

Enough said
Can you get the job done
All you need to worry
About is making me cum

We will see how far
This will go
But you got to be able
To do it sweet and low

Sweet Kisses

Sweet kisses like raindrops
Down my neck and you won't stop
Kiss my lips with your lips slightly parted
Chipping ice away from my cold heart
The warmth of your lips make the way
As your tongue enjoys play by play
With my nipple
As you trickle down
Down, Down, Down
Find my belly button
And lick it all around
You take a breath
I hear you sigh
You are waiting for me to reply
The answer to your question
Can you move on?
Your eyes look up at mine
I see in them my favorite song
I nod to you yes, to keep going
The anticipation is what you are showing
To kiss the other lips that you enjoy
They are your favorite toy
You place sweet kisses upon my lips
As you rub your hands across my hips
My clit and your tongue in a French kiss
As you put my mind in a subliminal bliss
Your sweet kisses can satisfy
My body, to you, I won't ever deny

Take Me From Behind

Let's discuss something
That's a true fact
When I have sex
I like it from the back
I like my hair pulled
I liked my ass slapped
When you take me from behind
Don't give me any weak crap
Don't come at me
Not knowing what to do
I will find someone to replace you
I need to feel your full weight
Don't be afraid to give it all
I want to hear the
Slapping of your balls
Grab my shoulders
Give it full force
Until I scream so loud
Make me loose my voice
Hit the bottom of this pussy
I want to feel you in my chest
As I put your dick to the test
Hope you can last long
I don't need a two-minute man
I don't need a dick
With a short life span

The Cougar

When I turn fifty
I'm turning into a cougar
No more fucking men my age
I'm only fucking men
Thirty years or younger
Men who ain't even old
Enough to rent a car
Men who ain't old enough
To buy alcohol
Even if they are they
Still need to show their ID
Twenty to twenty nine is
The age I'm looking for
Men wearing Tims
Or waiting in line for
The new J's to come out
Someone who is still depends
On their mama to wash their clothes
Don't bring me any man
Who is going though midlife crisis
Or a man who takes Geritol or
Have to rub down with BenGay
I definitely don't want
A man with grandkids
No, let his pants be sagging
And cornrows in his hair
Someone to fuck me so good
That I feel like I'm twenty
Someone to inspire me to
Start washing his clothes
And making home cooked meals

Wet Dreams by Tiffany Taylor

I want one that will come over
For a booty call in the middle of the night
Wear my ass out and then leave me
Panting, sweating and wanting more
Have a bitch stalking and looking
For his ass when he is not there
For his birthday I won't buy
Him a nice suit or new tools for his toolkit
But instead a new game or
Controller for his game system

Just Call me the Cougar

Stranger

Come to my room and let me show you a surprise
Lick your lips while you look into my eyes
I asked you here because I wanted someone to tame
There is no need for you to know my name

This is a one-time deal, just for fun
But it will be more if you can make me cum
Don't worry about a thing, my husband is gone
It will be a week before he comes back home

Now take my clothes off and start with my shirt
Now slowly ease on down to my skirt
Climb on the bed so I can tie your hands
I'm the one in control and in command

I cover your eyes with a blindfold
I like fucking better with eyes closed
I take your clothes off with such ease
I put my breast in your face 'cause I'm such a tease

My tongue takes a long lick down your chest
I make circular motions from east to west
I then take my tongue and run it across your abs
You want me untie your hands so you can grab

I whisper in your ear "No, I'm not done"
Now I'm about to make you shoot off like a gun
I head to the appetizer before the main course
Next, I'm going to ride your ass like a horse

Wet Dreams by Tiffany Taylor

My lips cover you until your dick hits my throat
I get wetter with each slow stroke
I run my mouth up and down your dick
Then, I hear you whisper "You're the shit!"

I stop sucking and climb up and on
I sit on your dick like it is my own personal throne
I start riding you with a nice slow grind
I can tell you're about to lose your mind

When I catch a good rhythm nice and fast
I slow it down to see how long you can last
Your eyes roll to the back of your head
And all we hear is the squeaking of the bed

I release in pleasure right before you cum
You once again ask to know my name
Instead of speaking, I suck you off until you cum
It's so good you roll over and suck your thumb

You are the first of many I plan to tame
And you will never know my real name
I might be putting myself in danger
But I love having sex with a total stranger

Untitled

My pussy throbs for you
Like a heartbeat at
The anticipation of new love
Like the complication of
The first time making love

At the thought of you
She starts to smile
I can feel her lips curl

At the sight of you
She begins to jump
As if she is waiting for
You to stroke her

At the touch of you
She begins to moisten
Like she is drooling in the
Hunger of wanting to taste you

The wetness drips
Down your face
Like water droplets
After a spring shower

As she waits for you
To enter her
Every time the heart
Beats faster
She jumps faster and faster

Waiting to explode

Wait Til' My Husband Leaves

Yes, I want you more that ever
And you make love a whole lot better
But we need to wait until it's time to play
Plan it for a perfect day
We have to wait til' my husband leaves
I'm staying home sick is what he believes
Don't wait another minute
Don't waste any more time
I want sex so good
That it will blow my mind
Come into the house
And I'll push you on the bed
And immediately start giving you head
I like to hear you moan and groan
Your dick in my mouth
Is where it belong
You say that's enough
It's my turn
Your hot tongue in my
Pussy is what I yearn
I'm tired of foreplay
I want less play and more
Putting in work
Your dick is what
I've been waiting to climb
On top and go for a ride
Ready to feel your dick deep inside
Once we get the bed shaking
The bed moving
I'm going to ride your dick off

Wet Dreams by Tiffany Taylor

Tonight what I'm proving
Is how I love when you
And I start grooving
Until I hear him say,
"Hey Babe"
I look up and find
My husband standing
In the door way

Wet Dreams

I feel your hands
Rubbing down my chest
As your fingers take the
Journey to my breast
You find my nipples and
Give them a pinch
Your lips start kissing
My neck inch by inch
While your hand makes
Its way between my legs
Put your fingers inside
Until I begin to beg
I moan and groan
As you fingered me gently
You feel my wetness
Your mouth finds
My waterfall
When I said, "Oooh!"
It was with a slur
No more fingers or lips
I want to feel you deep
Hit it so good
Put my ass to sleep
I call your name
And I say it loud
We are fucking so hard like
We're performing for a crowd
I didn't want it to end
Wanted it to last forever
Giving it to you
Is always my pleasure

Wet Dreams by Tiffany Taylor
As I'm about to cum
I start to scream
And woke myself up
In the middle of my wet dream
I dreamed about you
Your face invaded my sleep
I would rather dream
Your face I would rather keep
Tonight, I smiled in my sleep
As I thought of you
I would rather feel you
And your touches too

Wet Pussy

Drip, Drip, Drip
When it's excited
And you lick it right
You might get invited
To enter into a
World of pleasure
That will keep
Your dick locked in
Like its holding treasure
The wetter, the better
As she glistens and glows
Spread eagle so you can see
How my juices flows
Rub it with
Your fingers and hear
The squishy sound
Lick your lips
Before you go down
It gets wet enough
To soak the bed sheets
Hit the right spot
And it will skeet, skeet
You can tell when it's ready
Because it likes to shine
It likes when you take your time
Wet pussy will talk to you
It likes to speak in tongue
It prefers conversation with
Someone well hung
You can't resist
When it smiles at you

Wet Dreams by Tiffany Taylor
Thoughts of pussy
Get stuck in your
Mind like a tattoo

You Fit Me Like a Glove

I like the way you make love to my body
When I'm with you I can be completely naughty
In between our sessions my pussy will yearn
For time with her teacher. I'm here to learn
It's been a long time coming and I've waited for years
For someone to fuck me so good, it brings me to tears
Just thinking about you makes me wet
You put moves on me that I won't forget
I try not to think about what happened before
I just want you to fuck me til' I'm sore
Say my name and fuck me hard
You can have it all tonight if you play your cards
Hit it from the back and slap my ass
I wanna see how long you will last
Talk dirty to me and make me scream your name
I'm going to make you do the same
I wanna ride you on the couch
And feel you deep within
I need you to make me cum time and time again
It's like we are perfect for each other
We fit so right
I'll be calling that dick mine by the end of the night

You Have to Earn It

The vision he sees in his head
Is butt naked sex in my bed
He asked to pick me but that didn't work
Because I met him at the place
Yet I could still see the sneaky grin on his face

He tried to get me drunk to take advantage
But I'm telling you when it comes to drinking
I'm not average

We've only gone on one date, so...
What makes you think you are getting any
Lotion can be a man's best friend
I hope you have plenty

Just because you bought me dinner
Doesn't mean you are getting between the sheets
You better go home and beat your meat

You've done nothing to earn it
You don't even know my last name
Getting pussy is your only aim

But No. You will not have my legs up in the air
And have me stripped down to the bare

Have me bent over and hitting it from the back
Man, you must be smoking crack

This ain't free pussy
You can't get it when you want it

Wet Dreams by Tiffany Taylor

Your dick might be good but I will not be up on it
You will not be getting your dick sucked
Or your balls massaged
So to you motherfucker I say to you...bon voyage

You'll Never Get This Again

Let's get something straight
You've had your last time
To bask in the glory of this pussy
I mean the very last time
The truth is that
You actually get on my nerves so bad
That if I knew I could get away with it
I would push your ass off a cliff
Yet, I digress
I'm not going to do that
The sex was good
I will admit that
And you could have kept getting it
But instead you kept giving me reasons
That you couldn't come over
But that's okay
You simply let me stray
A little too far
For a little too long
And I found something better
Something to make me forget about you
Something so good that
Makes me call out my own name
He gives me what I need
He gives it to me so good
That when you do call and ask for it
I tell you that I'm good
And now that you know that I'm good
And that someone else is making
My pussy sing
You want to send texts

Wet Dreams by Tiffany Taylor
Back to back-to-back
What are you afraid of?
Yeah, I ride his dick
Backwards and forwards
You miss me knowing
That it could have been yours
But you had your chance
Pussy with no strings attached
Come on, you can't beat that
But I guess you made your choice
So go dive in a bottle of lotion to keep it moist

You're My Little Secret

Late nights coming over
Sneaking around
After dark sex treats
Acting like we don't know each other
But we do...
Every Thursday night is our playtime
That is when she has girl's night out

You cum over and fill my candy dish
With your sweetness and I enjoy every last drop
And I give you your special treat
A blow pop lollipop
The scent of us fills the air
And I wish I could put the scent into a spray bottle
To spray it when you are not there

Each time I have to send you back
Like a message in a bottle going back out to sea
Each time it gets harder and harder to let you go
Only I know that letting you go
Will sooth the pain I feel
The pain of not permanently having you
You don't belong to me
I'm not her

So I send you back to her
Two years of keeping this secret
When I could have had my own true love
And created my own joy
Instead of trying to take someone else
Stealing him from someone else

Wet Dreams by Tiffany Taylor
Keeping him my little secret

That Dick That Wouldn't Quit

Don't know what it's made of
But it's some powerful shit
Hell made me call it quits
Could be filled with energy drinks
Or something everlasting
At the end, it always leaves
Me asking
For more
It has the energy
To deliver with full force
Causing me to yell
Almost made me lose my voice
It keeps going and going
Every inch of my body
It was exploring
For us, there is no end
That dick had become my best friend

It has a mind of its own
Oh, if I had known
What it could do
I would have been prepared
For the nonstop tricks
Of his glorious dick
That can release itself and
Still remain hard
It has to be illegal
For him to remain standing
This long at attention
It's the baton that
Controls my pussy

Wet Dreams by Tiffany Taylor
It waves around and
She dances to whatever
The baton desires
It takes complete control

It has mind reminiscing
Sending shockwaves through
My body that are
Surely orgasmic
There's no stopping it
It is the best I ever had
Makes me loose all self-control
And it controls me
The dick that wouldn't quit

www.ingramcontent.com/pod-product-compliance
Lightning Source LLC
Chambersburg PA
CBHW072014060426
42446CB00043B/2464